# THE COMPLETE BOOK OF
# MUMMIES

## ALL ABOUT PRESERVED BODIES FROM LONG AGO

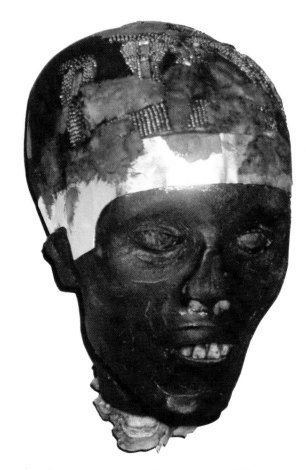

# Claire Llewellyn

HODDER
*Wayland*

an imprint of Hodder Children's Books

Produced by Roger Coote Publishing

Gissings Farm, Fressingfield

Suffolk, IP21 5SH, UK

First published in Great Britain in 2001

by Hodder Wayland,

an imprint of Hodder Children's Books

A CIP record for this book is available from
the British Library

Cover design: Victoria Webb

Inside design: Sarah Crouch

Editor: Alex Edmonds

Consultant: Dr. Bob Brier has spent more than 20 years studying
ancient Egypt and is one of the world's most respected
authorities on mummies. He teaches philosophy and Egyptology
at Long Island University in New York, USA.

Printed and bound in Portugal by Edicoes ASA

ISBN 07500 3019 4

Hodder Children's Books

A division of Hodder Headline Limited

338 Euston Road, London NW1 3BH

**Picture acknowledgements**
AKG London 24 top, 26, 28 bottom (Erich Lessing), 29 left (Erich Lessing),
30 top (Erich Lessing), 31 top, 40 bottom, 42 top (Erich Lessing); Ancient Art
and Architecture Collection 32 right (R Sheridan); courtesy of Ancient
Monuments Laboratory, English Heritage 39 bottom; British Museum front
cover inset; Camera Press 5, 8 (Viennareport), 11 top (Rachad El Koussy), 12
bottom (Viennareport), 13 top (Viennareport), 29 right, 30 bottom, 34, 35
bottom, 36 top, 41 bottom (NCNA); CM Dixon front cover main image, 11
bottom, 23 top, 27 top, 32 left, 33 bottom, 35 top; Corbis 38 (Reuters
NewMedia Inc), 42 bottom (Richard T Nowitz), 43 bottom (Kelly-Mooney
Photography); Impact 41 top (Christopher Cormack); MPM Images 9 (SNS
Pressebild); Rex Features 9, 12 top (SIPA), 13 bottom (SIPA), 37 bottom
(SIPA), 40 top (SIPA), 43 top; Robert Harding Picture Library 10 bottom
(Chris Rennie), 19 top (Gascoigne); Rog Palmer 39 top; Science Photo Library
10 top (Niedersachsisches Landesmuseum, Germany/Munoz-Yague), 16 top
(John Mead), 17 (Silkeborg Museum, Denmark/Munoz-Yague), 18
(Forhistorisk Museum, Denmark/Munoz-Yague), 19 right (Archaeologishes
Landesmuseum, Germany/Munoz-Yague), 19 bottom (National Museum,
Copenhagen/ Eurelios), 33 top (Philippe Plailly/Eurelios), 36 bottom
(Alexander Tsiaras), 37 top (Alexander Tsiaras); South American Pictures 20
top (Tony Morrison), 20 bottom (Chris Sharp), 21 top (Tony Morrison);
Stone 21 bottom; Werner Forman Archive 14 top (Greenland Museum), 14
bottom (Greenland Museum), 22 top (Musée Royaux du Cinquantenaire,
Brussels), 22 bottom (Egyptian Museum, Cairo), 23 bottom (Egyptian
Museum, Cairo), 25 top (Egyptian Museum, Cairo), 28 top (E Strouhal), 31
bottom (Egyptian Museum, Cairo). The map on page 8 is by Peter Bull. All
other artworks are by Michael Posen.

# CONTENTS

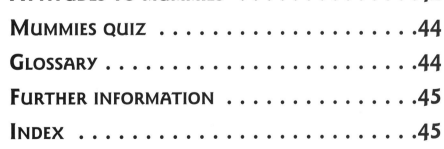

Words in **bold** are explained in the glossary.

# DISCOVERING A MUMMY

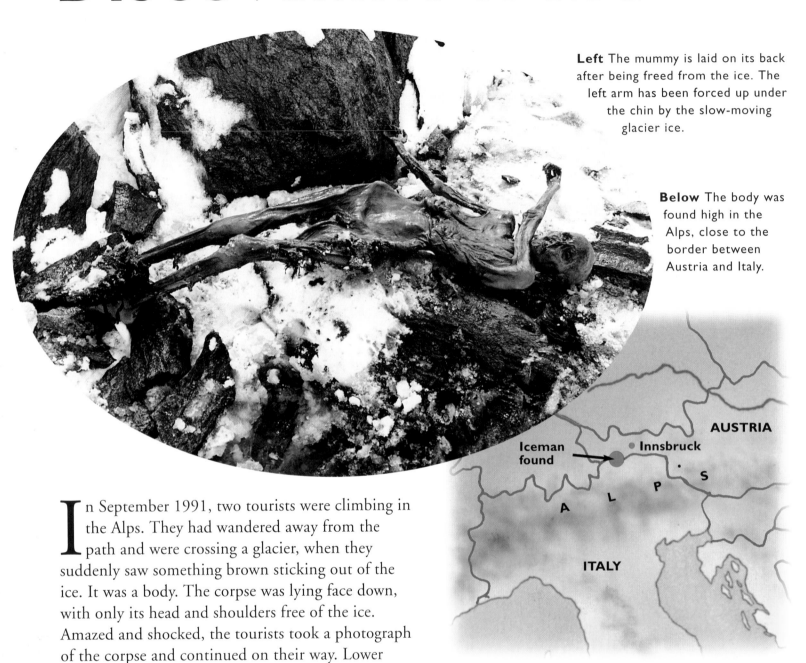

**Left** The mummy is laid on its back after being freed from the ice. The left arm has been forced up under the chin by the slow-moving glacier ice.

**Below** The body was found high in the Alps, close to the border between Austria and Italy.

AUSTRIA

• Innsbruck

Iceman
found

A L P S

ITALY

I n September 1991, two tourists were climbing in the Alps. They had wandered away from the path and were crossing a glacier, when they suddenly saw something brown sticking out of the ice. It was a body. The corpse was lying face down, with only its head and shoulders free of the ice. Amazed and shocked, the tourists took a photograph of the corpse and continued on their way. Lower down, they reported their find to the authorities, who thought it was probably the body of a mountaineer who had been caught in an avalanche years ago.

## Freeing the body

The next day, a police helicopter was sent to retrieve the body. As most of the corpse was buried in the ice, it had to be cut free with a **pneumatic** chisel. Meanwhile, several strange items were spotted on the ground nearby. There was a wooden axe with a metal blade, a small dagger, a wooden bow sticking out of

the ice, a few scraps of leather and hand-sewn clothing, and some bits of wood and dried grass. These were collected and taken away with the body to be examined by forensic scientists at the University of Innsbruck in Austria.

In the **dissection** room, scientists looked at the body. They saw immediately that it was not a recent avalanche victim, but a very old, mummified corpse. They handled it very carefully and placed it in a refrigerator until it could be examined by a local professor of archaeology.

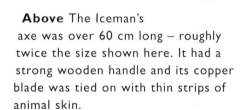

**Above** The Iceman's axe was over 60 cm long – roughly twice the size shown here. It had a strong wooden handle and its copper blade was tied on with thin strips of animal skin.

**Below** Scientists examine the Iceman. In time, the research team grew to over 100 experts.

# A 4,000-year-old sensation

The next day, the professor saw a shrivelled corpse on the dissection table. Next to the body lay the axe, the dagger and the other things that had been found with the corpse. The professor immediately saw that the mummy was about 4,000 years old – or older. It was a fully equipped prehistoric man. This was sensational: nothing like it had ever been found in modern times. The news spread quickly, and newspapers and TV companies from all over the world descended upon Innsbruck, wanting to learn more about the 'Iceman'. But the scientists' immediate task was to preserve the body. It had thawed out and was starting to decay. They decided to put it in a freezer. After all, it had survived perfectly well in a glacier for the past 4,000 years.

# WHAT IS A MUMMY?

**Above** This mummy was preserved in a **peatbog**. The man dates from the Iron Age (about AD 300), yet his hair, eyebrows and beard are almost perfectly preserved.

## A mummy tells all

The careful study of a mummy can reveal all kinds of information:
- The age and sex of the person
- His or her status in society
- How the mummy died
- At what time of year he or she died
- Any diseases or injuries suffered
- About childcare customs of the time
- About burial customs and beliefs
- About food and diet
- About clothes and textiles
- About weapons and tools
- About arts and crafts
- About ancient plants
- About ancient insects
- About the climate long ago

A mummy is a dead body that has been preserved. After death, a person's or an animal's body usually begins to decay and the soft parts, such as the skin and organs, soon rot away. But in mummies the decay does not take place. In many, this is because the body has been preserved on purpose by a process called embalming. Soon after death, the body is prepared and treated using chemicals. Embalming the dead was, and still is, often a mark of respect or a religious custom. In the past, many societies believed that preserving the dead person's body helped him or her in the **afterlife**.

But not all corpses are intentionally preserved. Some are preserved by accident – because the body was frozen, submerged in a peatbog or dried out in the desert or some other place where the natural processes of decay failed to take place. In some of these cases, the dead received simple burials; in others, they died very suddenly, and simply lay in the place where they fell.

**Right** Corpses can be preserved in dry conditions. This mummy was found in the desert of Southern Peru.

## Time passes

The dead lie undisturbed while time ticks by. Centuries come and go, wars are fought and forgotten and inventions push technology forward, changing our lives. And then suddenly, after hundreds or even thousands of years, a mummified body is found. This may be the result of a careful search in a historical site, or it may be a matter of pure chance, as with the Iceman in the Alps.

## Precious finds

Ancient artefacts reveal fascinating clues. Historians study jewellery, weapons and pottery for clues about the past. But a mummy was once a human or animal, and is much more significant than a piece of pottery. Mummies are packed with information; by studying them carefully, today's historians can learn about many aspects of life in the past.

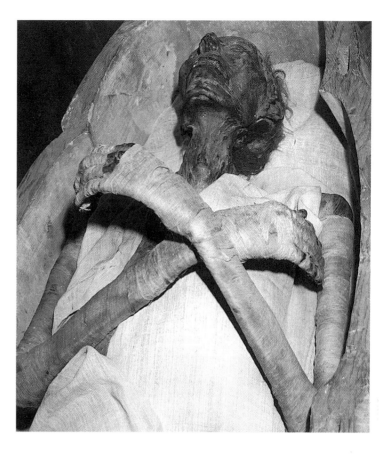

**Above** The world's most skilful embalmers were the ancient Egyptians. This mummy of Ramses II is 3,200 years old.

**Above** A skeleton is all that remains when the softer parts of the body have rotted away. Although bones and teeth reveal useful information, a mummy can provide more.

## Causes of decay

Human remains decay quickly because of the action of tiny **organisms**. These organisms thrive in regions which are moist, warm and rich in oxygen. Decay occurs most quickly in humid tropical conditions; it occurs hardly at all in deserts or frozen areas.

### DIG THIS!

• The word 'mummy' comes from a Persian word *mummeia*, meaning 'bitumen', a sticky substance that was sometimes used for **embalming**.
• The word 'embalm' means to rub with balsam, a thick sticky oil obtained from trees. There are different kinds of balsam. One of them is known as myrrh.
• Some ancient cultures, for example in Ecuador, preserved bodies by smoke-drying them.

# STUDYING THE ICEMAN

Since his discovery in 1991, the Iceman has been examined by many experts. They have established that the Iceman was male, and aged between 25 and 40 years old. He was rather short – about 1.6 m tall. Although all the hair had fallen out of the skin, enough of it was found on his clothes to confirm that it was dark brown and wavy. He probably also had a beard.

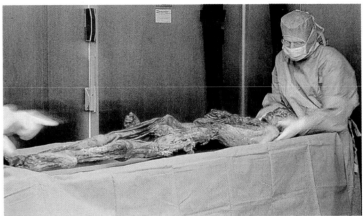

**Above** The Iceman is brought out of the freezer for expert examination.

There were several tattoos on his body: a set of blue lines on his back, a cross behind one knee and ankle, and stripes on the back of one leg. No one is sure why he had these tattoos, but since they are positioned by what archaeologists discovered were his stiffest joints, they may be connected with folk medicine. It was also discovered that the Iceman was injured when he died. X-rays have shown that he had broken ribs. To be in the mountains with such injuries suggests he may have been running away.

## The Iceman's clothes

Much of the Iceman's clothing was in fragments – just a few scraps of leather and bits of dried grass. This has been pieced together by experts. In all, his outfit comprised a fur cap, a deerskin tunic and leggings carefully sewn together with animal **sinew**, a leather loin-cloth, a knee-length cloak made of plaited grass, and leather shoes with plaited grass straps. Since the Iceman died by accident, historians can be sure that everything he wore was typical of his time because it was preserved by accident too.

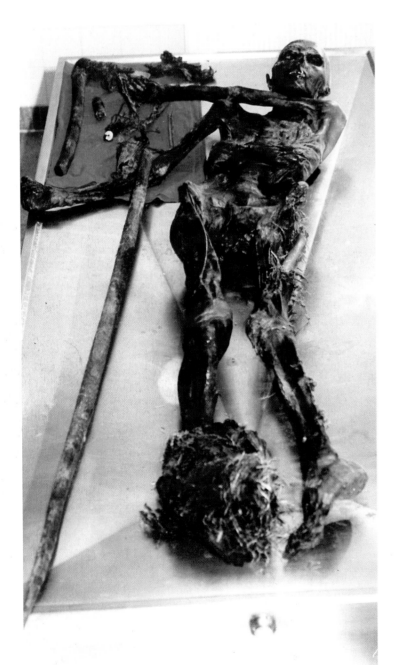

**Left** The Iceman was naked except for a grass-filled leather shoe on his right foot. Sadly, his left thigh was badly damaged by the pneumatic chisel that was used to free him from the ice.

## The Iceman's tools

The Iceman lived in Europe at the end of the Neolithic Period, a time when people were beginning to use metal instead of stones to make their weapons and tools. Although his dagger was made from flint, his axe had a copper blade. He was also carrying a half-finished yew bow about two metres long, a ball of twine made from tree bark, perhaps to use as a bowstring, and 14 arrows in a deerskin quiver. All the belongings were stowed in a leather rucksack with a wooden frame – the oldest rucksack in the world!

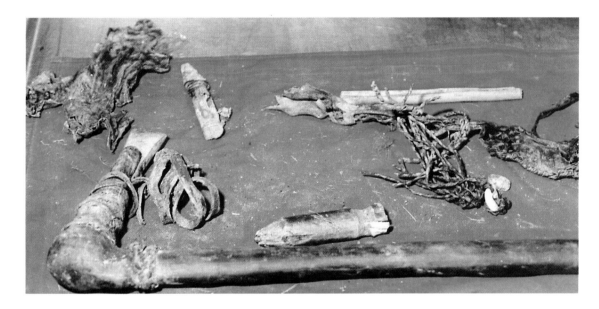

**Left** These are some of the Iceman's possessions: the axe and dagger, a small wooden tool used to shape and sharpen flints, a few scraps of leather and some bits of wood and twine.

**Below** This model of the Iceman gives an accurate impression of how he would have looked.

### DIG THIS!

- The Iceman's age has been confirmed as nearly 5,000 years old.
- He lived between 3300 and 3200 BC.
- Hairs on the Iceman's weapons show which animals he had hunted: red deer, ibex and chamois.
- The Iceman is so precious that he has been given two large freezers: one is just a spare in case the other breaks down!
- At first, the Iceman was taken out of the freezer for no more than 30 minutes at a time.
- The Iceman has been carefully conserved so that future generations of scientists can work on him.

## Working with wood

By analysing the Iceman's equipment, scientists have discovered that his bow, arrows, dagger handle and backpack frame were all made from different kinds of wood. Each wood was chosen for its particular qualities – its flexibility, lightness or strength. Since different kinds of trees and shrubs grow in different places, the Iceman must have deliberately searched out certain trees. He had a knowledge of his surroundings which was vital for survival in the Neolithic Period.

# IN THE FREEZER

Unlike the Iceman, some mummies preserved by ice were given a proper burial. Tombs have been found in Greenland and Siberia – two of the coldest parts of the world – where the corpses were frozen before they decayed and remained unchanged for hundreds or thousands of years.

**Below** This six-month-old baby is the best preserved of the Inuit mummies. The tiny body cooled quickly after death and had less time to decay.

**Right** The black lines on the forehead of this Inuit mummy are part of a tattoo. They were made, simply and painfully, by drawing a needle and stained thread through the skin.

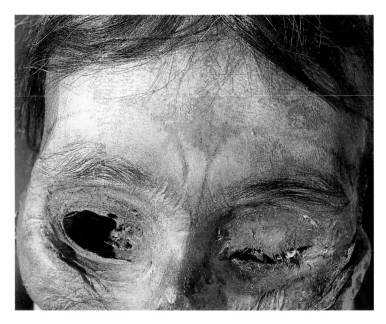

## Inuit tombs

Two brothers were out hunting in Greenland in 1972 when they noticed a curious pattern of stones on the ground. They lifted the stones, and found beneath them an underground chamber, containing the mummies of eight Inuit: six women, aged between 18 and 50, and two children – one about four years old, the other just six months old. It is not known how the eight people died. What is known is that soon after burial, due to a combination of very low temperatures and lack of moisture, their bodies were slowly mummified.

On expert examination, the mummies were found to date from about 1475, the time of Christopher Columbus. They had been buried according to early Inuit customs, ready for the long, cold journey to the Land of the Dead. All were wearing warm sealskin trousers and anoraks and high boots stuffed with grass – similar to garments worn in Greenland today. Their diet was also similar. The remains of food inside one of the women was found to contain traces of seal hair, reindeer meat, Arctic hare and ptarmigan feathers – all common foods in the Arctic today.

# A frozen tomb

Over 2,000 years ago, a people called the Pazyryk lived in the high, cold lands of southern Siberia. They were semi-**nomadic** herders and brilliant horsemen. They buried their dead with some of their possessions in deeply dug tombs underground. The graves, known as kurgans, were topped with a high mound of rocks.

In 1993, a team of Russian archaeologists found one of these ancient tombs. Inside was a log coffin, containing the mummified body of a woman. The organs had been removed from the body, and it had been embalmed with a mixture of grasses and herbs.

The woman was about 25 years old when she died, tall for her time and clearly important. Buried next to her were six harnessed horses that had been **sacrificed** for her to use in the afterlife. She was buried in clothes made of silk and wool, wearing beads and an intricate head-dress. Her skin was decorated with tattoos and she had with her a carved hand mirror made of polished metal. It is not known how she died.

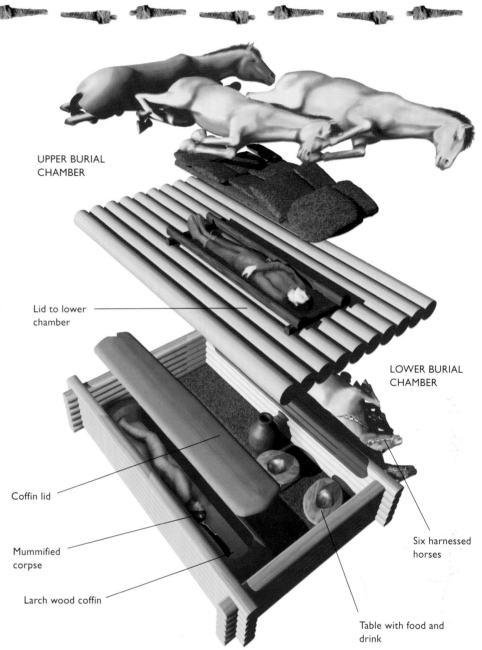

UPPER BURIAL CHAMBER

Lid to lower chamber

LOWER BURIAL CHAMBER

Coffin lid

Mummified corpse

Larch wood coffin

Six harnessed horses

Table with food and drink

**Above** Archaeologists found two burial chambers. The top one contained the skeletons of a man and three horses; the lower one contained the mummy of the Pazyryk woman.

## DIG THIS!

- One of the Inuit mummies was found to have high levels of soot in her lungs – far higher than those of city-dwellers today – from the seal-blubber lamp that burned and gave light in her home.
- Bees had built a hive in the Inuit grave. One bee was found, mummified, in the folds of a woman's clothes.
- When archaeologists discovered the Pazyryk tomb, they thawed it out gently with hot water. The whole process took several days.
- As the tomb thawed, the archaeologists could smell the plate of rotting horsemeat that had been left by the coffin for the next life.
- By testing food in the dead horses' stomachs, it was discovered that the Pazyryk burial had taken place in the spring.

## Cold as ice

The Inuit in Greenland and the woman in Siberia were preserved by different means. The Inuit lay in an underground hollow which was airy but bitterly cold. They were preserved by freeze-drying. By contrast, the Pazyryk tomb in Siberia must have been flooded by rain or melting snow, which then froze to form a block of ice. It remained frozen even in summer. The sun's heat did not penetrate the grave because of the rocks that were piled on top. The woman's body was embalmed when she died, but this would not have preserved it for long. However it did manage to preserve it until the grave froze in winter. By contrast, the dead horses had quickly decayed. There was nothing left of them but bones.

# STEEPED IN PEAT

**Above** It is in peatbogs like this that ancient corpses, such as Tollund Man, have been found perfectly preserved.

A body will be preserved if it happens to be buried in a peatbog. Peat is a mass of dark brown plant material. It forms over thousands of years from the remains of decaying plants in waterlogged ground. If a bog is drained, the peat can be cut, dried, and burned as fuel, giving heat for the oven and home. In many parts of the northern world, people rely on peat for fuel and, as they cut it, they sometimes find bodies preserved in the bog.

## Early bog bodies

The oldest bodies ever found were discovered in Florida, USA. They were the remains of early Native Americans, who lived about 7–8,000 years ago. The dead hunter-gatherers were placed on their side in shallow water, wrapped in grass mats and then covered with peat and wood. Although many of the bodies decayed, in some the brains have been found preserved and provide some of the oldest known human **DNA**.

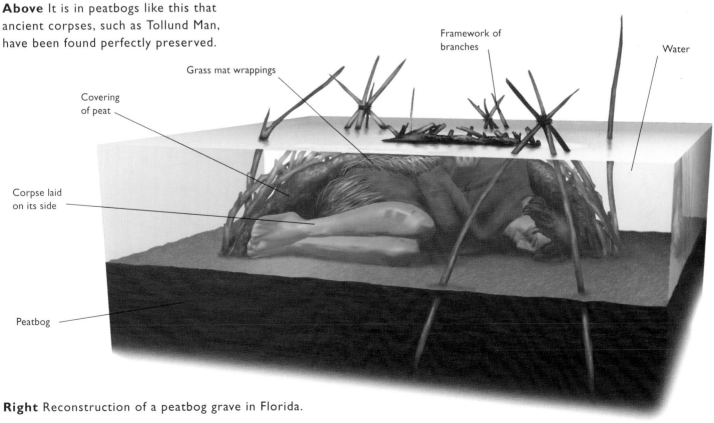

Framework of branches

Water

Grass mat wrappings

Covering of peat

Corpse laid on its side

Peatbog

**Right** Reconstruction of a peatbog grave in Florida.

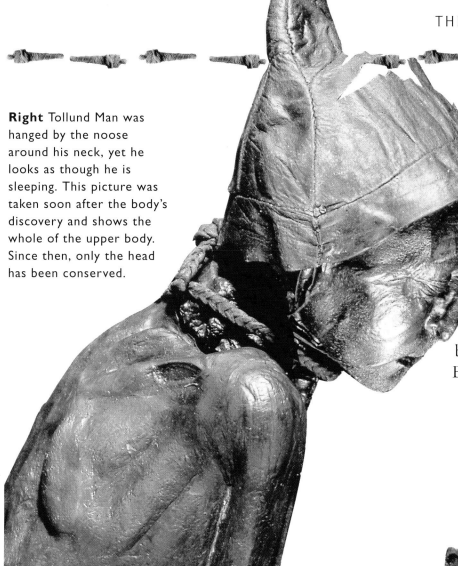

**Right** Tollund Man was hanged by the noose around his neck, yet he looks as though he is sleeping. This picture was taken soon after the body's discovery and shows the whole of the upper body. Since then, only the head has been conserved.

The day after the discovery, the mummy, surrounded by peat, was packed in a strong wooden box and transported to a museum. Investigation showed that the man, who was well over 20 years old, had been hanged by the rope around his neck. Remains of food inside his stomach indicated that his last meal had been a simple bowl of gruel made from a mixture of grains and seeds. Historians believe he may have been killed as a sacrifice to the Earth goddess.

## All about peat

A peatbog's preservative powers make it an archaeologist's dream. Organic remains, such as hair, skin, leather and wood, usually decay in the soil because of the action of bacteria. However, bacteria need oxygen and in a bog, layers of moss prevent oxygen reaching the lower layers. Also, the bog water contains acid from the surrounding soil. This **tans** the skin like leather, preserving it, and turning it a rich brown colour. If the acid is very strong, it will destroy the calcium in the bones so that they soften or disappear.

## Tollund Man

In 1950 a well-preserved corpse dating from the Iron Age (500 BC–AD 400) was discovered by two peat-cutters in a bog at Tollund in Denmark. It lay under two metres of peat. Many peatbog mummies had already been found in Denmark, but this one was especially well-preserved. The 2,000-year-old body was that of a man, naked except for a leather cap fastened under his chin, a belt around his waist and a twisted leather **noose** around his throat.

**DIG THIS!**

- Peat is an early stage in the development of coal – that 's why it burns so well.
- The men who discovered Tollund Man immediately called the police. They thought they had stumbled on a murder victim.
- Only Tollund Man's head was eventually conserved. It was soaked for over a year in different baths, including one of alcohol and another of wax.

# VIOLENT ENDS

Many peatbog mummies had violent deaths. Some, like Tollund Man, suffered injuries that suggest they were killed and buried as part of a religious ritual, perhaps as a sacrifice to the gods. Others were probably executed as a punishment for some crime, and were simply thrown into the bog.

## Grauballe Man

Two years after the discovery of Tollund Man, Danish peat-cutters found another mummy, this time in the village of Grauballe. It, too, was a naked man. Though the head and body had been slightly flattened by the heavy weight of the peat, it was still very well preserved.

The man was at least 30 years old at the time of his death. His body showed no signs of illness, but there was little doubt as to how he had died: his throat had been cut from ear to ear. He had also suffered broken bones and a heavy blow to the head. An investigation of his stomach showed that his death probably occurred in the winter, since the remains of his last meal contained no traces of summer or autumn fruits.

**Below** Grauballe Man died about 2,000 years ago. He is now on display in a museum in Denmark.

## 'The Grauballe Man'

The Irish poet, Seamus Heaney, was so moved when he saw the Grauballe Man that he wrote a poem about him. This is an extract from the opening of the poem.

As if he had been poured
in tar, he lies
on a pillow of turf
and seems to weep

The black river of himself.
The grain of his wrists
is like bog oak,
the ball of his heel

like a basalt egg.
His instep has shrunk
cold as a swan's foot
or a wet swamp root . . .

From *The Selected Poems of Seamus Heaney*, Faber and Faber, 1980.

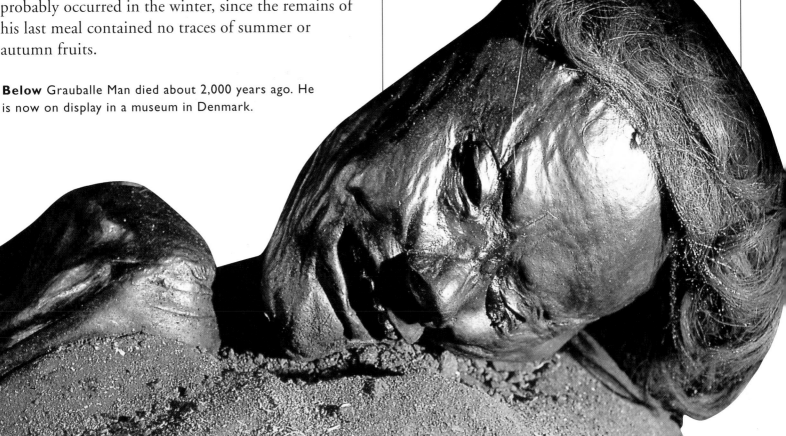

**Above** The skin on Grauballe Man's hands and feet was so well preserved that it was possible for police to take prints. These would have been enough to identify him, had he been a modern criminal.

Historians think Grauballe Man may have been killed as a human sacrifice. Like Tollund Man, he had recently eaten a gruel made of a mixture of seeds. Perhaps it was a special dish associated with a midwinter festival. Seeds symbolize the fertility of spring. This human death may have been seen as a way of hastening spring, and bringing bounty to the village.

**Above** The half-shaved head of the Windeby Girl suggests her death may have been punishment for adultery.

## DIG THIS!

- More than 2,000 bodies have been found in European bogs — most dating from 800 BC to AD 400.
- Conservationists soaked Grauballe Man in a strong bath of oak bark to complete the tanning process, then gradually dried the body and saturated it with oils.
- The seeds found in a mummy's food remains tell botanists which plants were growing in the area in the past.
- Watery places, such as bogs, were sacred to Iron Age people.

**Above** A bog body excavation site in Denmark.

## Windeby Girl

Another Danish peatbog mummy was found in Windeby bog. It was the body of a young girl about 14 years of age, who had lived 2,000 years ago. She too was naked except for a fur collar around her neck and a bandage tied tightly around her eyes.

Unlike the other two mummies, there was no sign of injury on her body. Historians believe that she was led out naked to the bog and held underwater until she drowned. A clue that supports this theory is the fact that one side of her head had been closely shaved: according to contemporary Roman writers, the punishment of an unfaithful wife was to have her head shaved in front of her family, and to be drowned in the local lake.

# BASKETS AND BUNDLES

Many mummies have been found in the coastal deserts and high Andes mountains of South America. This part of the world has been inhabited since about 1800 BC by many different cultures, including the Incas, whose vast 15th century empire stretched from Ecuador in the north to Chile in the south – a distance of over 4,000 km.

To the people of South America, preserving their dead was not only a way of honouring their family members, it was also profoundly religious. They probably believed that the mummies were a bridge between the world of the living and the world of the dead and might offer precious protection.

**Above** Many mummy bundles have been found in simple cord baskets that helped the corpse to sit upright. These were then placed in graves and surrounded by goods.

## DIG THIS!

• The fisherfolk on the coast of Chile were mummifying their dead 2,000 years before the Egyptians.
• The oldest mummy in South America dates from 5050 BC.
• The Incas mummified their dead kings and carried them through the streets on special occasions.
• The Inca civilization was destroyed in the mid-1500s when Spanish explorers invaded South America.
• In the 1880s hundreds of well-preserved mummies were found in a vast desert cemetery in Peru.

**Left** The mummies of these two adults and two children were discovered in the Atacama Desert, Chile, and date from 2500 BC. The corpses were stripped of their flesh, wrapped in cords and re-built with ash paste.

**Below** The corpses of this Inca mother and child sit alongside the remains of their dog. Many Inca families had working dogs which were often buried with their owners in case they could be of help in the afterlife.

## Sitting for eternity

In most mummies, the corpse was placed in a sitting position with knees up against the chest. The hands were placed over the face and the arms and legs tied in place. The corpse was then wrapped in reed matting or beautiful textiles. These may have helped to dry out the body by drawing off the body's fluids. Sometimes a false 'cushion' head or a fabric, wood or metal mask was placed on the mummy bundle, in the hope of protecting it from danger.

The mummy was then buried along with goods, such as clothes, jewellery, vases and tools, that would be of use to it in the afterlife. Clearly, the number and quality of goods placed in the grave were an indication of the dead person's wealth and standing. Some people were buried with gold and silver.

## Sacrifice of the young

The Incas practised human sacrifice. In times of drought or other crises, young children of about eight to twelve, were led up to the highest mountain peaks and sacrificed with their parents' approval. Their lives were a gift to the gods. Some of the bodies of these child victims have been found buried in the rocks, where they were freeze-dried by the cold mountain air.

## The oldest mummies

The earliest mummies date from about 5000 BC. They were made by prehistoric fishing people along the coast, who used an elaborate method of preservation. First, they stripped a corpse of its flesh and organs and tied the skeleton to a framework of sticks. Then they stuffed the body cavity with ashes and dried plants, covered it all over with ash paste and painted it. Finally, the skull was covered with a painted mask, and human skin and hair were attached.

In some places in later years, only the internal organs were removed, and the body was smoke-dried before being rubbed with oils, **resins** and herbs. In others, the mummies were more simply preserved by the natural conditions – the dry desert climate or cold mountain air.

**Below** The Atacama desert in Chile is the driest desert in the world. Corpses were naturally preserved there.

# EGYPTIAN EXPERTS

**Above** In Egyptian art, such as this 3,000-year-old papyrus painting, the Ba is represented as a human-headed bird.

The world's most famous mummies are those of the ancient Egyptians. Over thousands of years the people of this ancient civilization developed sophisticated techniques for embalming their dead. These artificial means of mummification were inspired by their religious beliefs and by their hot, dry desert climate.

## Religious beliefs

The way people prepare and bury their dead is often closely linked to their religious beliefs. The Egyptians believed that there was some kind of existence after death. They believed that a human personality was made up of several separate elements, and that two of these – the Ka, the spirit, and the Ba, the soul or life force – were needed to ensure eternal life.

At death, the Ka left the body, but it visited the tomb each morning to feed on offerings placed there by a priest. Preserving the dead body enabled the Ka to recognize and return to the correct tomb.

The Ba, represented as a bird with a human head, also left the body at the time of death but returned to it frequently, to use it as a perch. For the ancient Egyptians, the promise of eternal life depended on a home for the Ka and the Ba; it depended on a well-preserved corpse.

**Above** The Ka was represented by a pair of upraised hands.

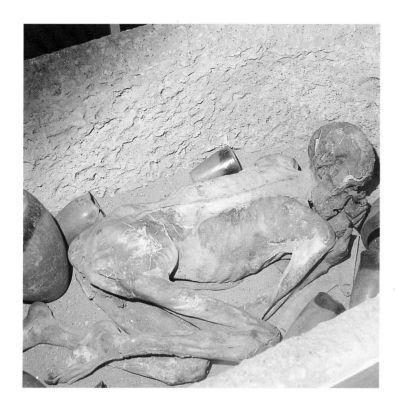

Egyptian society was the king or **pharaoh**. He was not only the most powerful person in Egypt, he was also thought to be a god. It was for the pharaoh, his family and other great nobles that the most sophisticated mummification was reserved.

**Above** Egypt's hot desert climate resulted in the natural preservation of many corpses buried in the sand.

**Below** This gold funeral mask was made for the pharaoh Psusennes I (1039-991 BC).

## Simple beginnings

The first Egyptian mummies were preserved quite naturally. A dead person was buried in a shallow grave in direct contact with the burning sand. The sun's heat and the dryness of the sand combined to **desiccate** the body's **tissues** before they could decay, while the fluids were absorbed by the sand.

In time, people wanted to provide a more comfortable grave, and more elaborate coverings and coffins. However, separating the body from the hot, dry sand resulted in its decay. The Egyptians' religious beliefs required a long-lasting, lifelike corpse. To achieve this, people had to find new ways of preserving the body and they began to experiment with artificial mummification. Not all of the early attempts were successful, but by 2600 BC true mummification was being successfully practised.

## Social standing

The same treatment was not given to all Egyptians. The complexity of the embalming process and the richness of the burial reflected the wealth and social standing of the person buried. At the apex of

# PREPARING THE BODY

**Left** The preserved corpse was placed inside a mummy-shaped coffin. This one dates from 100 BC.

There is no known Egyptian text giving the details of mummification. However, a Greek historian called Herodotus, who travelled in Egypt, wrote a full account of Egyptian embalming methods during the 5th century BC. Although this was long after mummification had reached its peak, modern historians believe it to be accurate.

## Cleaning the corpse

As soon as possible after death, the corpse was taken to the embalmer's workshop, which was known as the Pure Place. There it was stripped and placed on a board.

The first task was to remove the internal organs before they had time to decay. To remove the brain, a metal scoop was inserted into the skull through the nostril. This was used to mash the brain, which could then be extracted through the nose.

**Right** Preparing the body.

Next, a cut was made in the lower abdomen. The embalmer then reached inside the body to cut and free the intestines, stomach and liver. A second cut was made higher up so that the lungs could be removed. The heart and kidneys were left in place.

## Preserving the organs

The dead person's organs were washed, mixed with spices and dried with natron, a natural salt found in Egypt. They were then made into four separate parcels, and placed inside containers known as canopic jars, which were later put in the tomb.

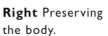

**Right** Preserving the body.

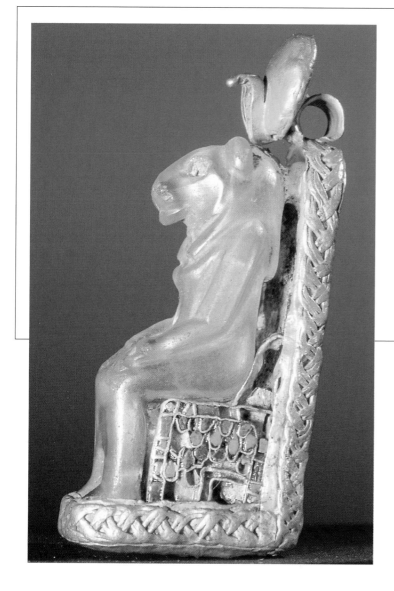

## Amulets

Amulets were magical charms that were believed to ward off injury and offer magical protection. In life, they were worn on necklaces and bracelets. In death, they were placed inside the linen strips that were wound around the mummy. Special spells were recited as they were put into position, such as this one to the mother goddess, Isis: 'You have power, O Isis! You have magic, O Isis! This amulet is a protection for the Great one. It will drive away those who would perpetrate evil against him!' (Spell 156, *Book of the Dead*)

**Left** This amulet, found in the tomb of a royal official, represents the lion-headed goddess Bastet, sitting on a golden throne.

## Wrapping the corpse

To restore the shrunken body to a more lifelike shape, the head, face, neck and other areas were plumped up with a packing of sawdust, linen, mud and sand. Linen pads were placed over the collapsed eyeballs, and the nostrils were plugged with resin. Finally, the body was wrapped in yards of linen strips, and pasted with bitumen, beeswax, precious oils and spicy, scented gums. In special spots between the bandages, the embalmers placed lucky charms called amulets, which they hoped would protect the dead.

## Preserving the corpse

The body cavity was rinsed out, rubbed with spicy resins and packed with natron. It was then placed in a bed of natron, which gradually absorbed the body's fluids. This process of **dehydration** took up to 40 days, and resulted in a withered, discoloured but flexible body, no longer affected by decay.

**Right** Washing the body prior to stuffing it.

**Right** Stuffing the body.

# READY FOR THE AFTERLIFE

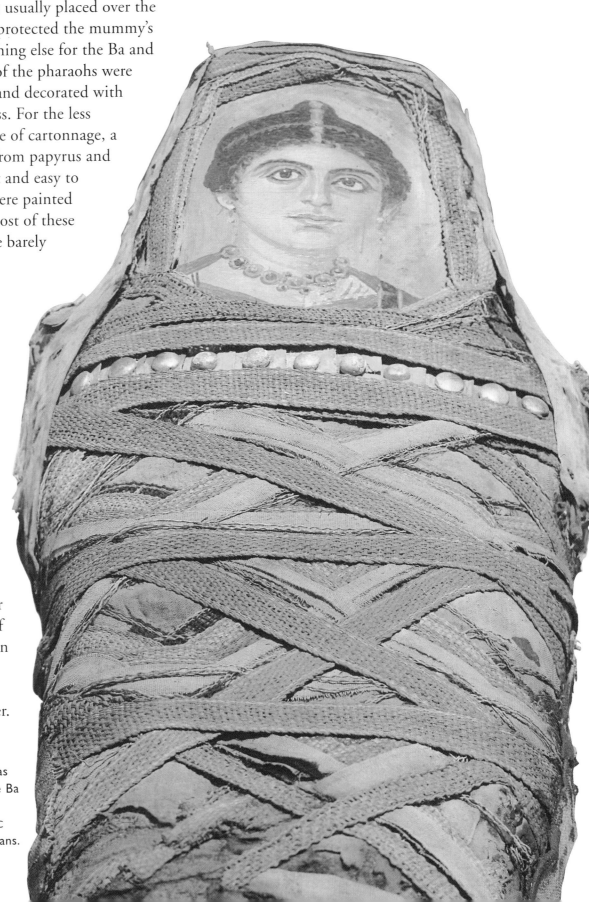

After the body had been embalmed and wrapped, a mask was usually placed over the head. This not only protected the mummy's face but also provided something else for the Ba and Ka to recognize. The masks of the pharaohs were made of solid gold or silver, and decorated with semi-precious stones and glass. For the less wealthy, the masks were made of cartonnage, a type of papier-mâché made from papyrus and linen, which was cheap, light and easy to paint. Although the masks were painted with portraits of the dead, most of these were highly stylized and were barely recognizable as real people.

## Into the coffin

The finished mummy and a portrait of the dead person were then placed inside a coffin. This protected it from the attentions of robbers and maybe even wild animals. The first coffins were plain wooden boxes, but later ones were made in the shape of a mummified body. For extra protection, the mummies of wealthy people were placed in two coffins or sometimes in a whole nest of coffins like a series of Russian dolls. The outer coffin was often painted with an idealized picture of the owner.

**Right** In many cases, a portrait was laid over the mummy to help the Ba and Ka identify the body. This portrait dates from about 300 BC when Egypt was ruled by the Romans.

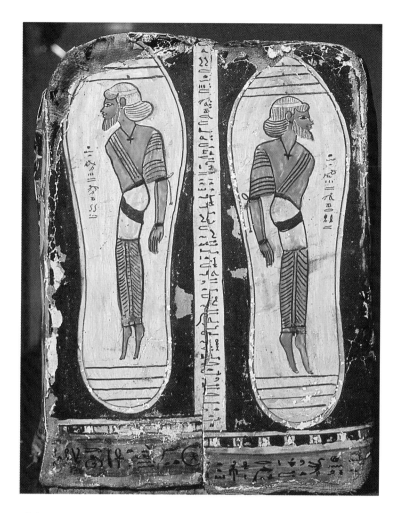

**Above** The base of this coffin, belonging to a pharaoh, has been decorated with a painting of feet. Under the feet are two prisoners who represent the pharaoh's power.

The sides of the coffins were decorated with pictures of gods and goddesses, and inscriptions in **hieroglyphs**. These were sacred Egyptian texts and were intended to help the dead in their dangerous journey to the next world. One such inscription reads: 'I shall not be afraid in my body, for words and magic shall overcome this evil for me. I shall see the Lord of Light, I shall live there. Make way for me.'

The mummy was then returned to the family, ready for the burial ceremony when it would be placed inside the tomb.

## Signs and symbols

Special symbols were painted on coffins and the walls of tombs. Egyptians believed that these magic symbols would protect the mummy until it came safely into the afterlife.

The scarab beetle was the symbol of Re who represented rebirth.

The symbol of the eye, known as the wedjat eye, represented healing.

A lotus flower was a symbol of life, death and rebirth.

This symbol, the ankh, is the Egyptian sign of life.

The falcon was a symbol of the sky-god, Horus.

### DIG THIS!

• Many coffins were mass produced. In most cases, the face painted on the coffin bore no resemblance to its owner.
• Egyptian hieroglyphs could only be read after 1822 when a French scholar called Jean-François Champollin discovered how to decipher hieroglyphs.
• A mummy was often laid to face east. That way it could see the sunrise, a symbol of rebirth.

# IN THE TOMB

When all the arrangements had been made for the burial, the mummy was taken by sledge to the tomb. Behind it, a funeral procession carried food and drink, furniture and personal possessions to place inside the tomb. A group of women followed on behind, waving their arms, weeping loudly, and throwing sand in the air. They were professional mourners who were paid good money to attend.

## The final ceremony

At the entrance of the tomb, the mummy was placed upright while a final ceremony, known as the Opening of the Mouth, was performed. During the ritual, a priest recited an **incantation**, while gently touching the mummy's eyes with an adze, a carpentry tool. Egyptians believed that by touching the wood of the coffin at these places, it would restore sense and movement to the corpse, enabling it to enjoy the afterlife.

**Below** The Opening of the Mouth was one of the most important funeral ceremonies. In this tomb painting, the priest performing the rite is wearing the mask of Anubis, the jackal-headed god of mummification.

## Grave goods

The coffin was laid in the tomb or lowered inside a stone **sarcophagus**, which was then sealed with a heavy lid. It was surrounded by all sorts of goods that might bring the mummy comfort and pleasure: food and drink, board games, musical instruments, clothes, make-up, jewellery, pieces of furniture, and even tiny models of brewers, bakers and agricultural workers who would work long and hard in the afterlife. The entrance to the tomb was then sealed with stones and faced with a layer of plaster.

## Tombs of the pharaohs

The tombs of the pharaohs were uniquely splendid. The first pharaohs were buried in chambers beneath huge stone pyramids, which were believed to form stairways for the kings to climb into the sky.

**Above** These grave goods, including jewellery and cosmetics containers, were discovered in a young woman's tomb. It was hoped that they would please her in the afterlife.

**Left** The pyramids at Giza. Pyramids were designed as tombs for pharaohs and were built from 2686–2160 BC.

## Spoilt mummies

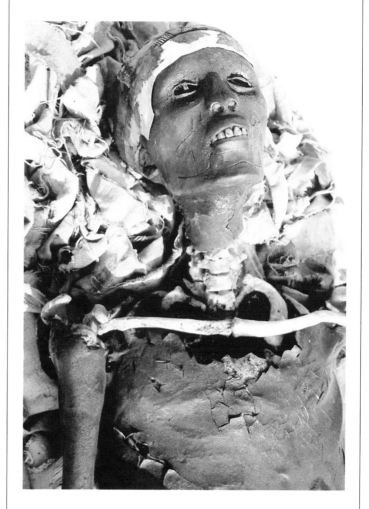

**Above** The pharaoh Tutankhamun's mummy was poorly preserved because of chemical reactions between the oils and resins.

To deter robbers, the pyramids were designed with secret entrances and false passages, and the burial chamber was sealed with granite but, even so, the tombs were looted of their treasure. Because of this, later pharaohs were laid deep in a cliff in a remote, guarded valley known as the Valley of the Kings. Yet despite this, all the tombs, bar one, were robbed.

**Below** A cutaway view of a pyramid, revealing the hidden entrances, false burial chambers and passageways designed to prevent looting.

Some mummies decayed in spite of the treatment they received. Sometimes this was due to chemical reactions between different embalming oils; sometimes they were damaged by greedy robbers; sometimes it was just poor embalming. As mummification became more popular in Egypt, embalmers were kept very busy. Any delay in starting work on a corpse would cause it to decay. Gradually standards began to slip. Sometimes the internal organs were not removed and only a thin coat of resin rubbed on to the skin. Modern examination has shown that mummies' heads sometimes broke off and limbs went missing, and body parts were muddled up. Anything could be concealed by bandages and a richly decorated coffin!

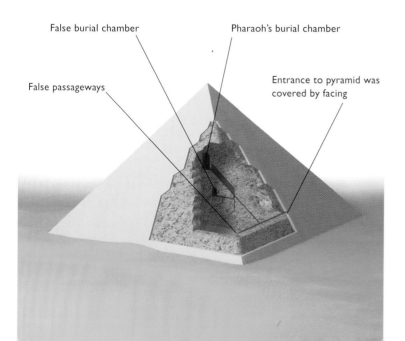

False burial chamber

Pharaoh's burial chamber

False passageways

Entrance to pyramid was covered by facing

# THE TREASURE OF TUTANKHAMUN

**Above** Below the heavy sarcophagus lid lay the first of three coffins. Made of cypress overlaid with gold foil, it shows the dead king with his arms crossed.

## Inside the sarcophagus

Deep inside the tomb sat the king's stone sarcophagus. Under the lid, beneath a number of shrouds, lay the first of three mummy-shaped coffins, each decorated with an image of the king. The first two coffins were made of wood, richly covered in gold foil. But the innermost coffin, the heaviest of the three, was made of solid gold, decorated with necklaces and carved with goddesses and gods.

**Below** Tutankhamun's head was the best preserved part of the body. It was clean shaven and wore a beaded linen skull-cap and a band of gold.

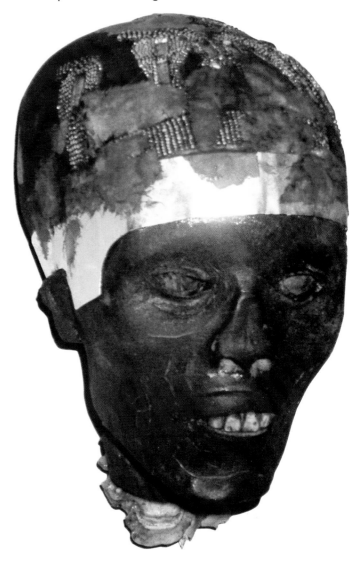

Tutankhamun became Pharaoh of Egypt in 1333 BC while he was still only a boy. He had ruled the country for just nine years when he suddenly died in mysterious circumstances and was buried in the Valley of the Kings. About 3,000 years later, in November 1922, a British archaeologist called Howard Carter found the entrance to a hidden tomb. It was the tomb of the pharaoh Tutankhamun.

## The glint of gold

The tomb was sealed with a plastered door, but Carter managed to dig a hole through, and peer in by the light of a candle. He later wrote, 'As my eyes grew accustomed to the light, details of the room within emerged slowly from the mist; strange animals, statues and gold – everywhere the glint of gold.' The tomb was crammed with furniture, chariots, golden **shrines**, gaming boards, jewellery and statues. It was the greatest treasure ever found.

## The mummy's curse

Howard Carter's patron, Lord Caernarvon, had been present at the opening of Tutankhamun's tomb. Three months later, he contracted pneumonia and died in Cairo after a mosquito bite became infected. Was his death the mummy's revenge for disturbing the pharaoh's rest? At the moment of Caernarvon's death, it was said, all the lights of Cairo went out! Howard Carter was scornful. He said, 'All sane people should dismiss such inventions with contempt.' Carter himself died 17 years later at the age of 64.

**Above** Howard Carter

This coffin contained the mummy of the king, covered with its famous gold mask. Unfortunately, the embalming oils used on the mummy had reacted badly with each other, reducing much of the body to soot. Only the face, protected by the mask, escaped damage. On examination, Tutankhamun was found to be about 1.63 m tall and slightly built. His head was clean shaven and his ears were pierced. The wisdom teeth in his jaw suggested that he had been about 18 years old when he died.

## The king's children

Two further mummies were found in a wooden box in a nearby chamber. They contained the corpses of two tiny children. One was the mummy of a foetus, only 25 cm long, which had been prematurely stillborn. The second child was slightly larger and had probably died at birth. The children are both believed to be girls, the daughters of Tutankhamun.

**Right** A chest ornament from the tomb of Tutankhamun.

### DIG THIS!

- Work on Tutankhamun's tomb was painstakingly slow as each item was carefully conserved. It took three years to reach the mummy. It took 15 years to clear the tomb.
- Tutankhamun had plenty of provisions for the afterlife: jars of wine and baskets containing different kinds of breads, meats, chickpeas, spices, honey and fruit.
- Huge crowds admired the treasures of Tutankhamun when they were exhibited in museums around the world. They are now on display in Cairo.
- The remains of Tutankhamun still lie in the stone sarcophagus in his tomb in the Valley of the Kings.

# ANIMAL MUMMIES

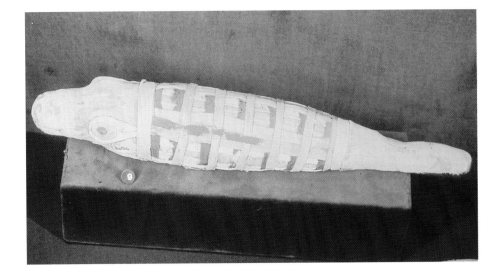

Animals have also been mummified. As with humans, mummification sometimes occurred by chance because the body was preserved before it had time to decay. But in ancient Egypt many animals were embalmed for religious reasons.

**Left** Dead cats were embalmed and wrapped, and had their faces painted on the bandages. They were placed in cat-shaped coffins.

**Above** Crocodiles in the River Nile were embalmed for religious reasons. They were believed to be the sacred representatives of Sobek, the god of the water.

## Sacred to the gods

The ancient Egyptians worshipped many different kinds of animals, including mammals, reptiles, birds and insects, because people associated them with goddesses and gods. Cats were sacred to the goddess, Bastet. Crocodiles were sacred to Sobek, god of the water. Falcons were associated with the sky-god, Horus. Scarab beetles were sacred to the sun god, Re. These and other animals were seen as the representatives of the gods, who could act on a person's behalf.

Sacred animals were mummified on an almost unimaginable scale; in fact, some of them were bred specially for mummification. Thousands upon thousands of corpses were prepared, bandaged and placed in coffins as richly painted as those made for humans. They were buried in special animal cemeteries, located in sacred sites.

## Mammoth mummy

Animal mummies are sometimes found perfectly preserved in ice. In the Arctic, the remains of woolly mammoths have been cut out of the **permafrost**, where they have been frozen for thousands of years. Mammoths are now extinct, but their frozen bodies have helped scientists to build an accurate picture of what the living animal must have looked like. A fully-grown male stood about 3 m high and had a domed head and humped shoulders. It had immense tusks, often turned inwards at the tips.

## Taxidermy

Taxidermy is the art of stuffing the skins of animals so that they look as lifelike as possible. Stuffed animals are not true mummies. They are usually little more than dried skin, complete with feathers or fur, that have been chemically treated against insects and decay. Taxidermy was very popular in the 18th and 19th centuries, when people became more interested in natural history, and flocked to public museums to see 'exotic' animals on display.

**Above** This well-preserved frozen mummy of a young mammoth was found in Siberia in 1977.

## Mummy or fossil?

Mummies and fossils are not the same. Mummies are preserved corpses. Fossils are the traces of animals or plants that are found in rocks. Fossils take millions of years to form. They are made from the hard parts of an animal's body, such as the shell, bones and teeth, which do not easily rot away. These parts are covered by layers of mud which over millennia turn to stone. The remains of the animal are also turned to stone, forming fossils. Much of what we know about life on Earth comes from fossils millions of years old.

**Below** A fossilized fish, now extinct, that lived millions of years ago.

### DIG THIS!

• In ancient Egypt, favourite pets were sometimes mummified and put in the tomb with their owners to keep them company in the afterlife.

• A single cemetery in Egypt was found to contain more than a million embalmed ibises (birds), each in its individual pot.

• Mummified animals are sometimes found under the floorboards of ordinary houses today. Cold draughts of air can dry dead mice.

• Woolly mammoths disappeared from the Earth about 11,000 years ago.

• One day it may be possible for scientists to clone a woolly mammoth by injecting the nucleus from a mammoth cell into the egg of a female elephant.

• Frozen mammoths are defrosted with hairdryers.

# UNWRAPPING A MUMMY

For those who are able to interpret them, Egyptian mummies contain fascinating information, not only about the individuals themselves, but also the place and time in which they lived. However, removing the bandages from a mummy is an irreversible act. Unless the procedure is supervised by experts, much of the evidence a mummy contains may be destroyed and lost forever.

## Early investigations

In the 18th century unwrapping mummies was a popular entertainment. People who travelled in Egypt brought home mummies as souvenirs. They invited their friends to ghoulish 'unwrappings', which lacked any scientific value. It was in the 19th century that the first genuinely scientific investigations took place. These took the form of a dissection and full anatomical examination of the mummy, followed by a chemical analysis. In spite of the scientists' good intentions, they were limited by the technology of the day.

## A modern approach

Today's scientists approach things differently. They have new tools at their disposal: X-rays and other kinds of sophisticated scanning equipment, tiny endoscopes that can 'see' inside the body, and powerful electron microscopes that magnify over 1 million times. Scientific attitudes have also changed. Modern-day scientists see it as disrespectful to cut open a once-living human being. They aim to achieve maximum knowledge with minimum damage by using non-destructive techniques. After all, mummies are valuable and rare.

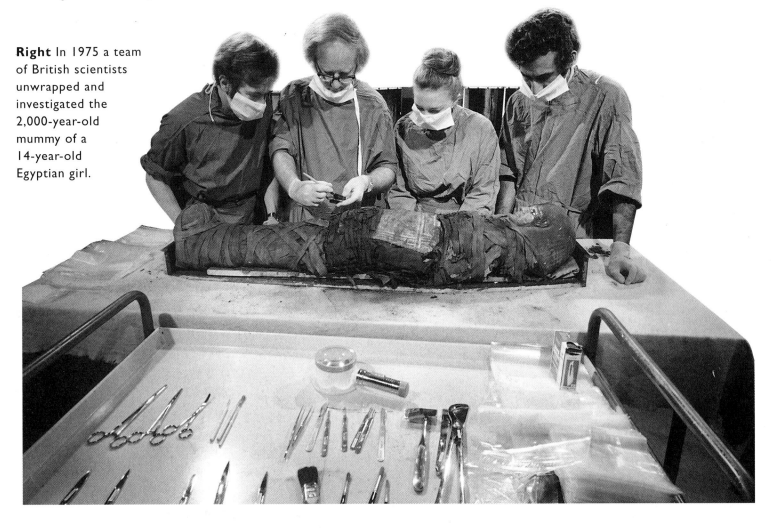

**Right** In 1975 a team of British scientists unwrapped and investigated the 2,000-year-old mummy of a 14-year-old Egyptian girl.

**Left** This reconstruction of a 5,000-year-old Egyptian burial site shows how a mummy may be discovered, surrounded by food and grave goods. For historians to have a fuller understanding, the entire context is very important.

## Team spirit

Unwrapping a mummy is a long and complex procedure. On the rare occasions when it is performed, a full team of experts is involved, reflecting many different lines of enquiry.

Pathologists, radiologists, chemists and dentists all set to work on the body. Botanists examine any plant material, such as pollen grains or seeds. Entomologists study any insects that are found. Textile experts examine the linen bandages and any threads that are present in the coffin. Archaeologists examine grave goods to see what they reveal. Every item is rigorously examined for the clues it may give about the dead person and the place and time in which she or he lived.

## Looking at teeth

A mummy's teeth can reveal how old the person was when he or she died. This is because the adult and wisdom teeth develop at well-known stages in a young person's life. Scientists can estimate an older person's age by the signs of wear and tear. The teeth of most adult Egyptians were very worn due to their coarse diet, particularly the bread, which contained small stones and sand.

Many Egyptians suffered toothache and dental disease. Although their healthy diet did not cause decay, the outer surfaces of the teeth wore down so quickly that the sensitive nerve was exposed. This must have allowed infection to enter the teeth, leading to abscesses, blood poisoning and even death.

**Above** Scientists make the first cut into the abdomen of a 2,000-year-old mummy.

## DIG THIS!

- It is generally possible to estimate the age of a child's skeleton to within one year, and an adult's to within ten years.
- Teeth are virtually indestructible. Tooth enamel is the hardest material in the body.
- Bones help to determine a mummy's sex. The average man's bones are bigger and heavier than the average female's, and the pelvis is a different shape.
- Bones can reveal the hardships of life, such as illness and malnutrition in the young, and arthritis in the old.

# TESTING, TESTING

Scientists conduct many kinds of tests on mummies. Sometimes the mummy is unwrapped; sometimes it remains intact. Scanning equipment can penetrate bandages, masks and even coffin cases to 'see' the preserved body inside. If a mummy has been unwrapped, scientists can introduce tiny cameras inside the body and take tissue samples. Microscopic and chemical analysis of the tissues often reveals evidence of disease and sometimes even the cause of death.

## Scanning the body

An X-ray produces a flat picture of the inside of the body. CAT (short for Computerized Axial Tomography) scanning, by contrast, is a way of taking hundreds of pictures of 'slices' of the body, which can be fitted together to form three-dimensional images. CAT scans make it possible to zoom in on any part of the body, inside or out, and examine it from different angles.

**Below** An Egyptian mummy about to undergo CAT scanning.

**Above** An X-ray photograph shows the secrets inside a mummy: the skull and bones of an Egyptian girl who died 2,000 years ago.

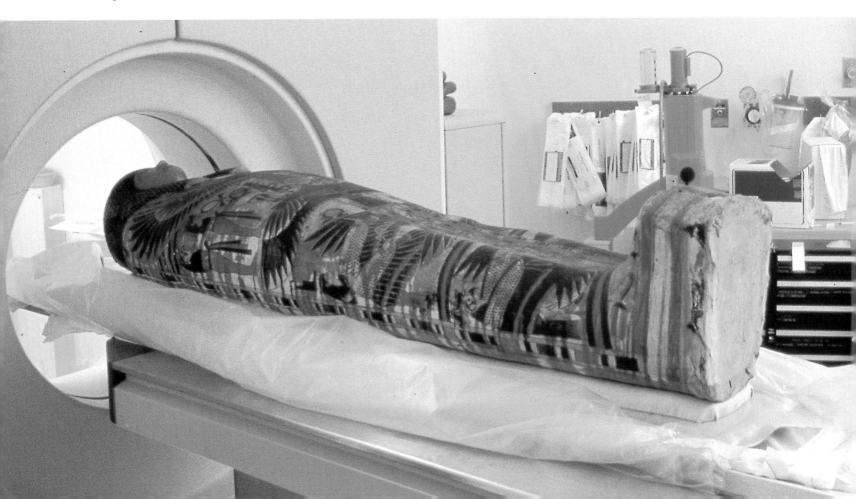

## Seeing inside

An endoscope is a long, narrow, flexible tube which can be inserted into a mummy through an opening such as the nose. An endoscope sends pictures to a video camera, allowing them to be viewed on a screen. This allows scientists to look directly at inaccessible parts of the mummy, such as the skull, windpipe and chest cavity, without having to cut it open. An endoscope can also be used to take small samples of tissue for closer examination.

## Looking at cells

Examining mummy tissue reveals information about common Egyptian diseases. For example, close analysis of lung tissue has revealed particles of sand in the lungs. This suggests that many Egyptians suffered from a condition called pneumoconiosis, which caused severe coughing and breathlessness. This came from breathing in dust or sand.

Tissue samples are taken from the mummy itself or organs in the canopic jars. The tissue is soaked in water so that it swells up and looks more lifelike. Then it is 'fixed' with chemicals so that it does not decay. Finally, the tissue is stained with dyes to reveal changes in the cells more clearly.

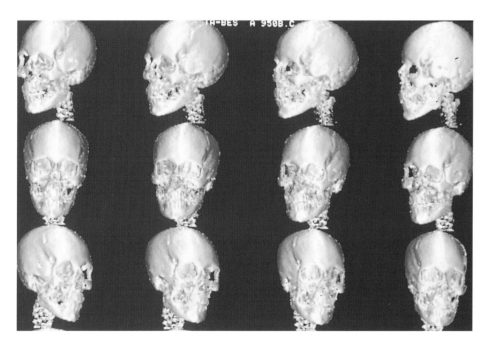

**Above** The CAT scans of a female Egyptian mummy have enabled scientists to produce this series of three-dimensional images of her skull. These were made without even having to open her coffin.

## Facial reconstruction

A sculptor can reconstruct a mummy's face from a model of the skull. First, about two dozen small wooden pegs are fixed to the skull to mark the average thickness of face muscles and tissue, which are then laid down in clay. The shape of the nose and mouth depends partly on clues in the shape of the skull. Of course, many details, such as spots, wrinkles, scars, eye colour and lip shape can only be guessed at but, in most cases, a facial reconstruction gives a very good idea of how a person would have looked.

**Right** An early stage in the reconstruction of a human face.

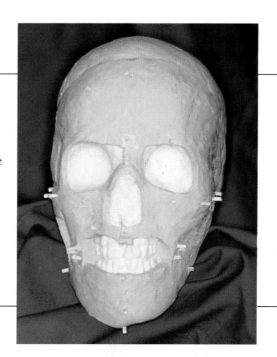

# HOW TO FIND A MUMMY

While some mummies are discovered by chance, others are the result of a long and determined search. The main problem for archaeologists who hope to find buried remains is knowing where to look. In some places burial sites are marked by stones or earthen barrows, which may last for thousands of years. But most tombs are gradually buried by sand or soil, and by modern roads and buildings. To find out where such tombs are likely to be found, archaeologists need to do research.

## A lucky find

Some archaeological finds are just down to chance. In 1993 archaeologists in Egypt made a major discovery. They came across a vast cemetery, dating from about 300 BC, filled with over 100 intact tombs. Early investigation suggests the cemetery holds up to 10,000 mummies, many of them covered with golden masks. This site – now known as the Valley of the Golden Mummies – was discovered when a donkey sank through the sand, and stuck its leg through the roof of a tomb!

## Armchair research

Archaeological research begins in libraries and public record offices which hold old maps and other ancient documents. Archaeologists study the meaning of old place names and read accounts of earlier fieldwork. This may help to identify an interesting-sounding site that can then be visited and explored.

## The lie of the land

Underground burial sites leave their mark on the landscape. They cause subtle changes in the depth of the soil, which are reflected by growing plants. The changes are often only visible from above. The low bumps and shallow hollows cast slight shadows, particularly in winter when the sun is low. These can show up clearly on aerial photos.

**Below** These mummies have lain untouched for over 2,000 years. They were found in the newly discovered tombs in the Valley of the Golden Mummies.

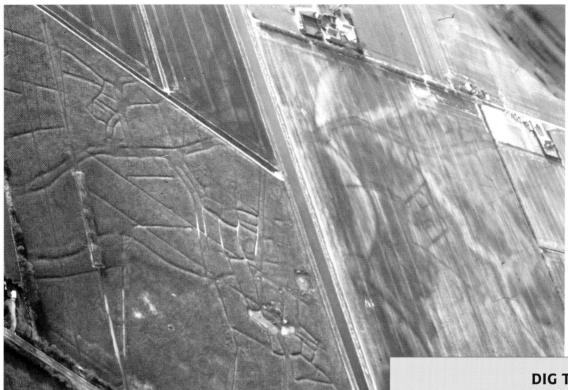

**Left** Archaeologists have the skill and experience to interpret aerial photographs. This view of Holbeach, Lincolnshire clearly shows the marks made by ancient buildings, streets and walls.

### DIG THIS!

- Many surveying instruments used by archaeologists were developed by geologists studying the structure of the Earth.
- Metal detectors are simple electromagnetic tools which sometimes detect buried treasure!
- Metal detectors and their owners are banned from archaeological sites.
- The excavation of the Valley of the Golden Mummies is likely to finish around 2010.

## Fieldwalking

Sometimes just walking over an interesting site can produce significant clues. This is known as fieldwalking and is particularly useful after heavy rain, when interesting objects have been cleaned and are more noticeable, and during winter when plants are low. A team of fieldwalkers pick up any archaeological remains they notice on the ground, such as pieces of pottery, flint, coins, or bits of building material. These help archaeologists to decide whether a site is worth the time and expense of an excavation.

## Sophisticated surveys

There are a number of sophisticated instruments that help to detect buried remains. These instruments are able to 'see' to different depths under the ground and detect different things. For example, something buried under the ground produces small changes in the strength of the Earth's natural magnetism. These can be measured using a magnetometer. Other instruments using electricity, radio and sound waves are also widely used in the field.

**Above** This archaeologist is using ground-penetrating radar equipment to detect evidence of historical remains.
**Left** Signals from the equipment are analysed by an image processor linked to a computer.

# MODERN MUMMIES

Mummies are not just remnants of the distant past. Embalming the dead is still performed as a means of preserving the corpse. Once used to secure the afterlife for ancient kings, embalming in the 20th century was used to preserve political leaders and international celebrities.

## Gone but not forgotten

The preserved remains of political leaders can continue to inspire their country. Vladimir Lenin, who led the Russian Revolution, died in 1924. His successors ordered doctors and scientists to find a way to preserve his body. They succeeded, and the embalmed body was put on public display in Moscow in spite of the objections of his widow. For 70 years, thousands of people – both Russians and tourists – visited the Lenin Mausoleum on Red Square to pay their respects. The body was monitored by embalmers who regularly changed his suit and bathed his body in a special chemical preparation to prevent decay. Still, despite their best efforts, the body has slowly deteriorated.

**Below** The preserved corpse of Russian revolutionary leader Vladimir Lenin has been on public display since his death in 1924.

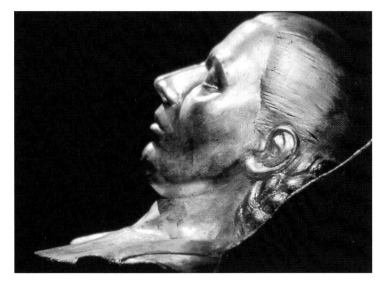

**Above** Eva Peron's preserved body was painted gold. Her political enemies feared that it would become a shrine.

## Stolen mummy

Eva Peron was an important public figure in the history of Argentina. As the wife of the Argentinian president, she was idolized by the country's poor. When she died from cancer at the age of 33, her body was embalmed and displayed in a glass coffin. Two million people filed past to pay their respects. Four years later, political enemies of her husband, fearful that her body would become a shrine, stole it and hid it in an Italian graveyard. In 1971 the body was exhumed and returned to Argentina, where – still perfectly preserved – it was buried in her family's vault.

## Mummies in Sicily

Underneath a church in Palermo, Sicily, is an underground cemetery containing about 6,000 mummies. The cemetery is a catacomb – a series of passages which are not only stacked with coffins and tombs but where mummies hang from the walls. The catacombs date back to about 1600, when the first mummy, a dead monk who had lived in the church, was embalmed by his fellow monks and laid to rest in a tomb. From that time on, all the monks were embalmed when they died, and it later became

**Above** A trio of mummies hangs from the walls in the catacombs of Palermo, Italy.

fashionable for professionals, such as doctors and lawyers, to have their body preserved in a similar way and dressed in their everyday clothes. Sicilians enjoyed visiting their dead relatives, often taking their young children along with them to have picnics down in the catacombs. This continued until 1920, when the last mummy was laid to rest. Now about 40 monks still live over the catacombs and look after all the mummies.

### DIG THIS!

- Following his death in 1953, Stalin's body was displayed alongside Lenin's. It was removed in 1961 when Stalin fell out of favour.
- At the time of Eva Peron's death in 1952 a pathologist had been on stand-by for a fortnight to embalm her.
- The great Italian opera singer, Enrico Caruso, was embalmed and put on show for five years after his death.
- In Salt Lake City, USA, you can now pay to have a relative embalmed, using methods very similar to the ancient Egyptians.
- Other famous mummies include the Chinese leader, Mao Tse-tung, the Vietnamese politician, Ho Chi Minh, and an ex-president of North Korea, Kim Il-sung.

### Living dead

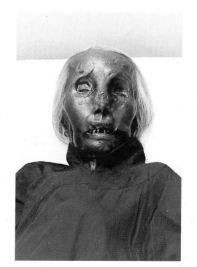

There are many weird and wonderful stories about mummies. This Chinese woman is said to be a 'natural' mummy. The story goes that for several days after she died, her body oozed dark liquids, then dried out and was perfectly mummified. Her family decided against burying the corpse, preferring for it to 'live' with them in her old room at home.

# ATTITUDES TO MUMMIES

**Above** In the 14th century, powdered mummy was widely prescribed. It was believed to have great powers of healing.

Throughout the ages, mummies have meant different things to different people, and have been handled with both great respect and deep irreverence. Thousands of years ago, a mummy was considered as a passport to eternal life, but since then it has also been regarded as a symbol of healing, horror and death.

## Mummies as medicine

In Europe during the Middle Ages there was a lively trade in Egyptian mummies. Powdered mummy was believed to have great powers of healing, and was one of the most commonly prescribed drugs. It sold for such high prices that foreign merchants fell over themselves to grab a share in the profit. Many of them traded in this commodity, ransacking ancient Egyptian tombs, and breaking mummies into pieces.

## Mummies in museums

By the 18th century, beliefs in the healing properties of mummies had begun to fade. By now, people were beginning to travel more widely, and were buying mummies as souvenirs. These attracted great interest and were regarded as collectable curiosities by museums and private individuals.

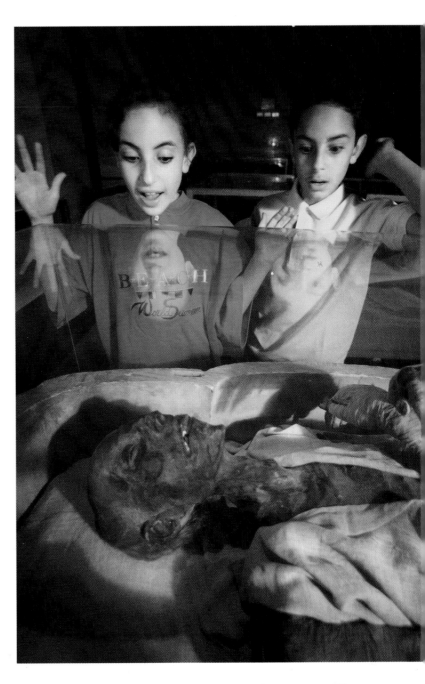

**Above** Mummies still have the power to fascinate us. They are some of the most popular museum exhibits.

**Above** In the Hammer film *The Mummy* (1932) Boris Karloff starred as a mummified priest brought back to life by an archaeologist. The film was so popular that it has been re-made twice.

## Mummies as fuel

Mummies were not always so highly valued in their own country. During the 19th century, the great stock of mummies in Egypt was used for fuel for the steam boilers of railway engines on the Cairo to Khartoum line! The ancient resins used as a coating on the mummies meant they burned extremely well.

## Mummies at the movies

With the invention of cinema, mummies entered the movies. The angry mummy disturbed from its sleep was the subject of *The Mummy*, a 1932 horror film starring the actor Boris Karloff. The film proved so popular that, not only did dozens of imitators follow on its heels, but it was re-made in 1959 and again in 1999. In the 1950s, in *Abbott and Costello Meet the Mummy* (1955), the mummy was used as a comic character alongside the two popular comics of the time.

**Below** This mummy seems strangely out of place in a souvenir shop in Seattle, USA. It is the preserved corpse of a man who had been shot.

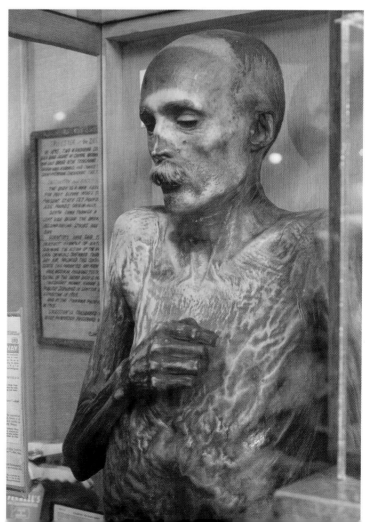

---

### DIG THIS!

- As a medicine, powdered mummy was often mixed with herbs to make it taste better.
- Mummies were once recommended for ailments such as bruises, fractures, abscesses, epilepsy, ulcers and coughs.
- Powdered mummy was once used to make brown pigment for artists. The colour was known by the Latin name *Caput Mortuum*, meaning 'dead head'!
- In 1997, the US Postal Service issued four stamps commemorating classic cinema monsters. One of them was The Mummy.

# MUMMIES QUIZ

Can you select the right answers to these questions? (They are all in the book.) To check if you are correct, see the end of the quiz.

1  *How old was the Iceman?*
a  400 years old
b  4,000 years old
c  40,000 years old

2  *In which of these places might a body be preserved?*
a  A cave
b  A desert
c  The sea

3  *Who were the Pazyryk?*
a  Inuit fishermen
b  Archaeologists
c  Siberian herders

4  *How did Tollund Man die?*
a  He was strangled
b  He starved to death
c  He drowned in a peatbog

5  *What effect does peatbog water have on the skin?*
a  It destroys it
b  It cracks it
c  It tans it like leather

6  *What was Grauballe Man's final meal?*
a  Roast duck
b  A gruel made from seeds
c  A fruit salad

7  *Where was the Inca empire?*
a  South America
b  Florida
c  Denmark

8  *How were corpses first preserved in Egypt?*
a  They were buried in a peatbog
b  They were covered in plaster
c  They dried out in the sand

9  *What is natron?*
a  A strong-smelling resin
b  A kind of salt
c  A long strip of linen

10  *What did the scarab beetle symbolize?*
a  Healing
b  Re-birth
c  Kingship

11  *Where were the first pharaohs buried?*
a  In a cemetery
b  In the Valley of the Kings
c  Inside the pyramids

12  *Who found the tomb of Tutankhamun?*
a  Boris Karloff
b  Lord Caernarvon
c  Howard Carter

13  *Where have mummified mammoths been found?*
a  In the Arctic ice
b  In Egypt
c  In rocks

14  *Why did Egyptians suffer from tooth decay?*
a  They ate too many sweets
b  Their teeth were worn down by stones in their bread
c  They didn't brush their teeth

15  *What is an endoscope?*
a  A scanning machine
b  A tool for cutting
c  A long narrow tube used to look inside a mummy

16  *What helped to discover the Valley of the Golden Mummies?*
a  Aerial photographs
b  A donkey
c  A magnetometer

17  *Who was Eva Peron?*
a  The wife of a president of Argentina
b  A Sicilian monk
c  A Russian revolutionary

18  *How was powdered mummy used in the Middle Ages?*
a  As fuel
b  As a drink
c  As a medicine

Answers: 1 b, 2 b, 3 c, 4 a, 5 c, 6 b, 7 a, 8 c, 9 b, 10 b, 11 c, 12 c, 13 a, 14 b, 15 c, 16 b, 17 a, 18 c

# GLOSSARY

**afterlife**  Life after death.

**amulet**  A charm worn or carried to ward off evil.

**dehydration**  When the water is removed from something.

**desiccate**  To dry.

**dissection**  To cut something up in order to be able to study it.

**DNA**  Molecules found in the cells of humans and some animals.

**embalming**  To stop something decaying by preserving it.

**hieroglyphs**  Pictures that ancient Egyptians used to stand for words and sounds.

**incantations**  Magic spells or charms that are repeated.

**nomads**  People who live by moving from place to place to find new food sources.

**noose**  A rope with a knot in it that tightens as the rope is pulled.

**organisms**  living plants or animals that are made up from one or several cells.

**peatbog**  Waterlogged ground consisting of peat – decayed plant matter.

**permafrost**  Soil below the topsoil that remains frozen all the time.

**pharaoh**  Egyptian king.

**pneumatic**  Something that is powered by compressed air.

**resins**  Sticky substances that some plants make.

**sacrifice**  When a person or animal is killed as an offering to a god.

**sarcophagus**  A stone coffin.

**shrine**  A place that becomes a focus for worship of a god.

**sinews**  Tough, string-like fibres that connect muscles to bones in a body.

**tan**  To turn something into leather by beating it repeatedly.

**tissues**  The groups of cells from which plants and animals are made.

# FURTHER INFORMATION

## Web Sites

**The Animal Mummy Project**
http://www.animalmummies.com/

**How to Make a Mummy**
http://www.nationalgeographic.com/media/tv/mummy

**Face to Face with Mummies**
http://www.discovery.com/news/features/mummyfaces/
mummyfaces.html

**Ice Mummies**
http://www.pbs.org/wgbh/nova/icemummies/

**Mysterious Mummies of China**
http://www.pbs.org/wgbh/nova/chinamum

## Books to Read

*Exploring the World of the Pharaohs*
Christine Hobson, Thames & Hudson, 1990
Adult book with mummy information.

*Eyewitness: Archaeology*
Jane McIntosh, Dorling Kindersley, 1994
Colourful, informative book.

*Eyewitness: Mummy*
James Putnam, Dorling Kindersley, 1993
Comprehensive guide to mummies.

*The Archaeologist's Handbook*
Jane McIntosh, Bell & Hyman, 1986
Reference book about modern archaeology.

*The Complete Tutankhamun*
Nicholas Reeves, Thames and Hudson, 1995
The Full story of the discovery of the tomb.

*The Man in the Ice*
Konrad Spindler, Orion Books, 1994
The fascinating story of the discovery of the Iceman.

*The Mummy's Tale*
Ed. Dr A R David and Dr E Tapp, Michael O'Mara
Books Ltd, 1992
The unwrapping and analysis of a mummy.

# INDEX